FRENCH PAINTINGS

FROM THE COLLECTIONS OF

MR. AND MRS. PAUL MELLON

AND

MRS. MELLON BRUCE

TWENTY-FIFTH ANNIVERSARY EXHIBITION

1941 - 1966

NATIONAL GALLERY OF ART

WASHINGTON

FOREWORD

THE NATIONAL GALLERY OF ART has been exceptionally fortunate in having the support of two generations of collectors. Permanently on view are the works of art assembled by Mr. Andrew Mellon. These are among the most important paintings and sculpture ever brought together by one person. Now, temporarily on view, are also the 19th and 20th century French paintings acquired by Mr. and Mrs. Paul Mellon, and Mrs. Mellon Bruce. This catalogue indicates the magnitude and comprehensiveness of their collections. That they have been willing to make this loan emphasizes their support of the institution their father founded—a support which over the years has been manifested in many ways.

We museum directors are apt to take for granted the willingness of collectors to live without their works of art. Yet as everyone knows who has lent a cherished treasure, to be deprived of a beloved painting, or drawing, or piece of sculpture represents a real sacrifice. The removal of an entire collection is far worse. Having persuaded Mr. and Mrs. Mellon and Mrs. Bruce to allow us to hold this exhibition to celebrate our 25th anniversary, I feel toward them a certain sense of guilt. I assuage my conscience by the thought of the pleasure these pictures will give thousands of visitors. Nevertheless, I cannot forget the temporary defacement of many beautiful rooms. Therefore, I want particularly to express the gratitude of the National Gallery of Art to these three collectors who have so unselfishly made possible our exhibition.

JOHN WALKER
Director

INTRODUCTION

PRIVATE COLLECTIONS HAVE THEIR OWN PHYSIOGNOMIES, which obviously reflect the tastes and attitudes of those who assemble them. It is almost a miracle, therefore, that this anniversary exhibition, although composed of two quite distinct collections, nevertheless presents a perfect unity. While it is true that Mrs. Mellon Bruce and Mr. and Mrs. Paul Mellon have devoted themselves to the same general era, they have each favored different aspects within that period, so that their collections—far from duplicating each other—actually complement one another in the most felicitous way. Brought together here for the first time, they form an ensemble of a magnitude the equal of which it is impossible to find anywhere in private hands.

There is, of course, a basic difference between a museum collection and one that is gathered by an individual. Whereas a museum should try to achieve a general representation of every trend and every artist of consequence, the private collector can more freely indulge his preferences. The museum director must go about his purchases more or less systematically and may even have to pass up opportunities because, for the sake of a balanced selection, he must first of all try to fill whatever gaps there may be; the private collector, to the contrary, has an unrestricted choice, even the choice to chart his own course and to be as arbitrary as he wishes. He may decide to assemble a comprehensive survey of a given period or style, or he may concentrate on a few favorite artists; he may endeavor to bring together a comparatively small group of works typical of their authors, or he may want to spread out and include in his collection works outside the mainstream, provided they give him pleasure. In the last analysis it is this pleasure, the desire to own a work of art, to live with it, to contemplate it again and again which distinguishes the private collector from the museum official.

The two collections exhibited here are comprehensive enough to represent every major artist (and even some minor ones) from Corot to the aged Bonnard and the young Picasso, thus affording an exceptional panorama of French art over a period of some one hundred years, yet they are also sufficiently eclectic to reveal preferences for certain masters. This in itself is evidence that these collections do not coldly aim at a hypothetic equilibrium but instead reflect their owners' search for works with which they feel special affinities. Indeed, no one can love all the artists of a given period to the same degree, yet it often takes both courage and wisdom to show favoritism in the choice of masters or of works. However, such an attitude is not only the privilege of the private collector, it actually provides the distinctive element of his collection. Among the great collections of the past, the best remembered are usually those that allowed personal accents, that revealed the human being behind the masterpieces he had assembled.

Collecting is a kind of disease and thus, to some extent, evades rational examination; it has no connection with ordinary needs, yet may take hold of mind and soul to a degree where there is no escape from it. The fatal symptom of the true collector is his strong acquisitive and possessive instinct, this constant urge to own which is aroused whenever he sees an object that moves or excites him. He rarely reaches a point of saturation and will continue to buy even though he may lack room properly to display his purchases. As long as there are temptations and as long as his circumstances allow, he will be ready to succumb; however, the significant thing is that he succumb with discrimination.

Unlike any other disease, collecting yields the most wonderful rewards. The joys of discovery are combined with the ordeal of decision, the pangs of hesitation with the delights of certitude; the whole gamut of frustration and excitement is encompassed, but above all are the tremendous and indescribable pleasures once a coveted object has been secured. Possession not only enriches the owner's experience and enjoyment, it also enables him to share his happiness with others, with friends and the general public, as is the case in this instance.

It is no secret that collecting in the field of French Impressionism and Post-Impressionism has become increasingly difficult because of the scarcity of outstanding works as well as the fierce competition among the few who are able to vie with each other for the rare masterpieces still available. While this situation has no bearing on questions of quality, it is an important factor if one wishes to appraise pertinently the collections assembled by the son and daughter of Andrew

Mellon. Indeed, the works shown here in such profusion have not been picked from a plentiful supply, for times have changed since the days when Albert Barnes or Chester Dale could leisurely make their choices from among abundant offers. Not the least admirable aspect of the collections exhibited here is that it should have been possible at all to assemble such an excellent representation of France's greatest modern masters and, incidentally, secure for this country many a work that does not have its equal in Europe.

Collecting today has frequently become a compromise between what one wants and what one can obtain. Compromises, however, are dangerous because they tend to impair the criterion of quality. Both Mrs. Mellon Bruce and Mr. and Mrs. Paul Mellon have preferred to be patient rather than to make concessions. As a matter of fact, it would have been difficult for them to have done otherwise since, after a certain point, a collection begins to take care of its own development. Once a given standard has been set—and here it was of the highest order—it maintains itself almost automatically insofar as inferior objects simply will not fit among the works already assembled. Masterpieces tolerate only masterpieces around them.

Mrs. Mellon Bruce's initial venture into the field of modern art consisted of the purchase, some twelve years ago, of the famous Molyneux collection with its emphasis on small canvases of exquisite charm and unusual mastery. To these she has, over the ensuing years, added a number of important works of larger dimensions, such as Monet's sparkling *Garden at Vétheuil,* Cézanne's shimmering *Riverbank,* and several particularly well-selected paintings by Renoir and Pissarro. Lest it seem that she has not been as active as her brother, it should be noted that she has taken a lively and generous interest in the collections of the National Gallery and has on numerous occasions elected to make notable purchases for the Gallery.

Mr. and Mrs. Paul Mellon for many years devoted their main attention to English painting between 1700 and 1850, and built one of the most representative and distinguished records anywhere of this generally overlooked period. It has been said of their collection that it "is not an art historian's check list; it is a rare, personal probing of a neglected era, and the resulting assemblage is both as inform- ative as it is refreshing." When they turned their attention to French art, Mr. and Mrs. Mellon did not, of course, venture into a similarly neglected field but found themselves confronted with numerous rivals. This prompted them to adopt a policy so discreet that many of their major purchases either have totally escaped public attention or at least have not been directly associated with them. As a result, this exhibition abounds in surprises, not only for the layman but even for those well acquainted with the hectic art world of today.

Among the most outstanding paintings in their collection is a group of superb canvases by Manet the like of which even few museums can boast; a magnificent series of beach scenes and seascapes by Boudin that reveal him as the great master he is (only when seen in such an excellent choice does he assume his true stature); an astonishing array of works by Monet through which one can follow his evolution from solid shapes to fluid masses; a unique cluster of rare paintings by Monet's friend Bazille who is still not sufficiently appreciated; an overwhelming row of small panels by Seurat in addition to his *Lighthouse at Honfleur,* a recent acquisition which was probably the only large oil by the artist that could still be obtained (incidentally, the National Gallery itself does not own any paintings by Seurat). Such an enumeration, however, does not do justice to this collection in which there are a great many other masterpieces, by Cézanne, Degas, Gauguin, van Gogh, Renoir, Sisley, their predecessors and followers.

As the catalogue of this exhibition reveals, for the last two decades there has scarcely been an important auction sale in New York or London or Paris at which Mr. and Mrs. Mellon have not successfully bid for some remarkable works. But their name was never announced and the new purchase was whisked away to their home where it could be seen only by some privileged few. This may sound like the plot of a mystery novel, yet now that the result of this policy can be appraised it becomes obvious that the avoidance of all publicity has borne splendid fruit. In complete silence but with untiring persistence they have assembled a collection of incredible proportions. What is even more important: they are adding to it constantly.

Were it not that the anniversary of the National Gallery had prompted the son and daughter of Andrew Mellon to abandon their customary reserve and to display their treasures publicly, the range of their collections would still not have been divulged. It is important, nevertheless, for the visitor to remember that he is introduced, for this special occasion, to a group of works that represents but a selection from these two collections which continue to grow and expand.

Few people seem to realize that pictures should grace a home and be truly loved in the intimacy of private surroundings before they reach the walls of a public institution. As a matter of fact, the artists who painted these canvases seldom dreamed—and were even more seldom encouraged by their contemporaries to dream—of museums. Rather than think of anonymous masses, they merely hoped that a few enlightened collectors would appreciate their work. It is almost as if their paintings needed a period of incubation during which silent fervor would bring about the full maturation of their virtues and thus ready them for a public gallery. But a collector can do even more than provide warmth of admiration; he can gather companions for his prizes to better set them off and to achieve an over-all unity. This is exactly what has happened in these two collections.

There can be no doubt that Pissarro would have been happy to see his canvases next to those by the revered Corot; that Boudin and Jongkind would have been pleased that their pupil Monet was here their neighbor; that Courbet would have welcomed the company of Renoir; that Degas may have been amused to share the limelight with his admirers, Mary Cassatt and Forain; that van Gogh would have been deeply moved to be close to Gauguin and Seurat; that Lautrec would have been flattered to be hung near his idol Degas; that Monet would have rejoiced to see Cézanne so extraordinarily well represented; that Bonnard and Vuillard would not only have been delighted to appear side by side but would also have been touched to figure in the wake of Monet, Gauguin, and Cézanne.

Indeed, this exhibition achieves a threefold purpose: the artists are shown at their very best and, in this assemblage, enhance one another, displaying to the greatest advantage one of the most fertile periods of French culture; the visitors are being offered a rare treat which comprises many masterpieces not previously seen in this country, and the National Gallery is honored by an exceptional show which proves that the generosity of its founder lives on in his children.

JOHN REWALD

PAINTINGS

CAMILLE COROT (1796–1875)
1 · *River Scene with Bridge, 1834*
9⅞ x 13½ in.

CAMILLE COROT
2 · *Landscape at Mornex (Haute Savoie)—Morning, 1840–50*
15¾ x 24 in.

CAMILLE COROT

3 · *Peasant Women Chatting in a Courtyard, c.1870*
18 x 15⅛ in.

CAMILLE COROT

4 · *Young Girl Reading, 1868–70*

12⅝ x 16⅛ in.

GUSTAVE COURBET (1819–77)

5 · *Portrait of Mademoiselle Jacquet, 1857*

32 x 25½ in.

GUSTAVE COURBET
6 · *Calm Sea, 1860*
21¼ x 25 in.

G Courbet. 1865

GUSTAVE COURBET

7 · *Boat on a Beach, Trouville, 1865*
36⅛ x 25⅞ in.

JOHAN JONGKIND (1819–91)
8 · *The Towpath, 1864*
13½ x 18½ in.

EUGÈNE BOUDIN (1824–98)
9 · *The Fourteenth of July Regatta at Honfleur, 1858*
15⅞ x 23⅛ in.

EUGÈNE BOUDIN
10 · *The Beach at Trouville, 1863*
13⅝ x 22⅜ in.

EUGÈNE BOUDIN

11 · *Jetty and Wharf at Trouville, 1863*

13⅝ x 22¾ in.

EUGÈNE BOUDIN

12 · *On the Beach, c.1865*

15¼ x 24½ in.

EUGÈNE BOUDIN

13 · *Beach Scene, 1862*

12¼ x 18⅝ in.

EUGÈNE BOUDIN

14 · *Bathing Time at Deauville, 1865*

13⅝ x 22¾ in.

EUGÈNE BOUDIN
15 · *Beach Scene at Deauville, 1865*
16½ x 25½ in.

EUGÈNE BOUDIN
16 · *Beach at Trouville, 1864–65*
$10\frac{5}{8}$ x $19\frac{1}{4}$ in.

EUGÈNE BOUDIN

17 · *The Beach at Trouville, 1864*

10¼ x 18½ in.

EUGÈNE BOUDIN
18 · *The Beach, 1877*
4⅜ x 10¼ in.

EUGÈNE BOUDIN
19 · *Woman Washing, Trouville, 1863*
6¾ x 10 in.

EUGÈNE BOUDIN

20 · *Ships and Sailing Boats Leaving Le Havre, 1880*

$35\frac{1}{2}$ x $51\frac{1}{4}$ in.

EUGÈNE BOUDIN
21 · *The Outer Harbor of Le Havre, 1888*
35½ x 51⅜ in.

EUGÈNE BOUDIN

22 · *A Country Villa, 1885*

12¼ x 15½ in.

EUGÈNE BOUDIN

23 · *The Seine at Argenteuil, c.1866*

11¾ x 18½ in.

EUGÈNE BOUDIN

24 · *Horses Outside a Stable, c.1884*

9½ x 12½ in.

CAMILLE PISSARRO (1830–1903)
25 · *A Road in Louveciennes, 1870*
19¾ x 24 in.

CAMILLE PISSARRO

26 · *The Hedge, 1872*

14⅞ x 18 in.

CAMILLE PISSARRO

27 · *Orchard in Bloom, Louveciennes, 1872*

18 x 21½ in.

CAMILLE PISSARRO

28 · *Young Peasant Girls Resting in the Fields near Pontoise, 1882*

25¾ x 32⅛ in.

CAMILLE PISSARRO

29 · *Young Peasant Girl, 1881*

28½ x 22¾ in.

CAMILLE PISSARRO

30 · *The Artist's Children, Cocotte and Bébé, Playing on a Rug, 1883*
12¾ x 16⅛ in.

CAMILLE PISSARRO

31 · *Seated Peasant Woman, 1885*

28¾ x 23⅝ in.

CAMILLE PISSARRO
32 · *Charing Cross Bridge, London, 1890*
23 ½ x 36 ¼ in.

CAMILLE PISSARRO

33 · *Hampton Court Green, 1891*

20½ x 28 in.

CAMILLE PISSARRO

34 · *The Artist's Garden at Eragny, 1898*

29 x 36¼ in.

CAMILLE PISSARRO

35 · *The Gardener—Old Peasant with Cabbage, 1883–95*

31½ x 25¼ in.

CAMILLE PISSARRO
36 · *Gray Weather at Eragny, 1899*
23¾ x 28¾ in.

CAMILLE PISSARRO

37 · *Place du Carrousel, Paris, 1900*

21½ x 25¾ in.

ÉDOUARD MANET (1832–1883)
38 · *A King Charles Spaniel, c.1866*
18 x 15 in.

ÉDOUARD MANET

39 · *Tama, the Japanese Dog, c.1875*

24 x 19½ in.

ÉDOUARD MANET

40 · *The Plum, c.1877*

29⅛ x 19½ in.

ÉDOUARD MANET

41 · *Promenade—Portrait of Madame Gamby in the Artist's Garden at Bellevue, 1879*
36½ x 27½ in.

ÉDOUARD MANET

42 · *Rue Mosnier, Paris, Decorated with Flags on June 30, 1878*

25½ x 31½ in.

ÉDOUARD MANET

43 · *George Moore in the Artist's Garden, c.1879*

21½ x 17¾ in.

ÉDOUARD MANET

44 · *The Melon, c.1880*

18⅜ x 22¼ in.

ÉDOUARD MANET

45 · *Flowers in a Crystal Vase, c. 1882*

12⅜ x 9¼ in.

ÉDOUARD MANET

46 · *The Beach at Boulogne-sur-Mer, 1869*

12¾ x 25¾ in.

EDGAR DEGAS (1834–1917)
47 · *Self-Portrait with White Collar, c.1857*
8¼ x 5⅞ in.

EDGAR DEGAS
48 · *Steeplechase—The Fallen Jockey, 1866*
71 x 59½ in.

EDGAR DEGAS

49 · *At the Races, c.1878*

7½ x 9⅝ in.

EDGAR DEGAS

50 · *Portrait of the Artist's Aunt, the Duchess de Montejasi-Cicerale, c.1868*
17¾ x 14¾ in.

EDGAR DEGAS

51 · *Portrait of Madame Julie Burtin, 1863*

28¾ x 23½ in.

EDGAR DEGAS

52 · *Ballet Dancers, gouache and pastel, c.1877*

12½ x 11 in.

EDGAR DEGAS
53 · *Dancers at the Old Opera House, pastel, c.1877*
8 x 6¼ in.

EDGAR DEGAS
54 · *Race Course: Before the Start, 1878–80*
15½ x 35 in.

EDGAR DEGAS

55 · *The Dance Lesson, 1880–85*

15 x 34¾ in.

EDGAR DEGAS
56 · *Conversation, 1885–95*
19¾ x 24 in.

EDGAR DEGAS

59 · *Jockey in Blue on a Chestnut Horse, c.1889*

10½ x 8¼ in.

EDGAR DEGAS
60 · *Dancers at the Studio, 1889–95*
22¼ x 32½ in.

EDGAR DEGAS

61 · *Dancers Backstage, c.1890*

9 x 6¾ in.

HENRI FANTIN-LATOUR (1836–1904)

62 · *Grapes in a Bowl with Carnation, c.1880*

11⅞ x 18⅛ in.

HENRI FANTIN-LATOUR

63 · Grapes in a Basket and Apples, 1880

11 x 15 in.

HENRI FANTIN-LATOUR

64 · *Flowers, c.1885*

17¾ x 17 in.

STANISLAS LÉPINE (1836–92)
65 · *Landscape with View through Trees*
6½ x 10⅞ in.

STANISLAS LÉPINE

66 · *Bridge on the Seine, Paris, 1869*

15¾ x 21¾ in.

STANISLAS LÉPINE

67 · *The Dock at La Villette, Paris*

20⅛ x 36 in.

PAUL CÉZANNE (1839–1906)

68 · *Harvest, c.1877*

18 x 21¾ in.

PAUL CÉZANNE

69 · *Houses in Provence, c. 1880*

25½ x 32 in.

PAUL CÉZANNE
70 · *Boy in a Red Waistcoat, 1893–95*
35¼ x 28½ in.

PAUL CÉZANNE

71 · *Riverbank, 1895–98*

28¾ x 36½ in.

ALFRED SISLEY (1839–99)
72 · Street at Sèvres, 1872
15½ x 23½ in.

ALFRED SISLEY

73 · *Flood at Port Marly, 1872*

18 x 24 in.

ALFRED SISLEY

74 · *Wild Flowers, c.1875*

25¾ x 19⅞ in.

ALFRED SISLEY

75 · *Meadow, 1875*

21 ¼ x 28 in.

ALFRED SISLEY

76 · *White Frost at Marly, 1876*

14⅞ x 21⅝ in.

ALFRED SISLEY

77 · *Avenue of Chestnut Trees Along the Seine at Saint-Cloud, 1878*

20½ x 24¾ in.

ODILON REDON (1840–1916)
78 · *Pond in Les Landes, c.1880*
13 x 15¾ in.

ODILON REDON

79 · *Village by the Sea in Brittany, c. 1880*

9⅞ x 12¾ in.

CLAUDE MONET (1840–1926)
80 · *Bazille and Camille—Study for "Le Déjeuner sur l'Herbe,"* 1865–66
36⅝ x 27⅛ in.

CLAUDE MONET

81 · *The Cradle—Camille with the Artist's Son Jean, 1867*

45¾ x 35 in.

CLAUDE MONET

82 · *Ships at Anchor on the Seine, 1872–73*

21½ x 24 in.

CLAUDE MONET

83 · *The Bridge at Argenteuil, 1872–74*

23¾ x 31½ in.

CLAUDE MONET

84 · *The Bridge at Argenteuil on a Gray Day, c.1876*

24 x 31⅝ in.

CLAUDE MONET

85 · *Woman with a Parasol—Madame Monet (Camille) and Her Son, 1875–78*
39¼ x 32 in.

CLAUDE MONET

86 · *The Artist's Garden at Vétheuil, 1880*

59¼ x 47⅜ in.

CLAUDE MONET

87 · *Poppies at Giverny, 1885*

23¼ x 28½ in.

CLAUDE MONET

88 · *Cliffs at Pourville, 1882*

23½ x 39¼ in.

CLAUDE MONET
89 · *The Artist's Garden at Giverny, 1900*
35¼ x 36¼ in.

CLAUDE MONET

90 · *Waterloo Bridge, London, at Sunset, 1904*

25¾ x 36½ in.

CLAUDE MONET
91 · *Waterloo Bridge, London, at Dusk, 1904*
25 7/8 x 40 in.

BERTHE MORISOT (1841-95)
92 · *Young Woman in a Straw Hat, 1884*
21¼ x 17¼ in.

BERTHE MORISOT

93 · *The Artist's Sister, Madame Edma Pontillon, 1869*
21¾ x 18⅛ in.

BERTHE MORISOT

94 · *The Harbor at Lorient, 1869*

16½ x 22 in.

BERTHE MORISOT
95 · *The Harbor at Lorient (with the Artist's Sister Edma), 1869*
17 x 28¾ in.

BERTHE MORISOT

96 · *Young Girl with an Apron, 1891*

25½ x 21¼ in.

ARMAND GUILLAUMIN (1841–1927)

97 · *Pissarro's Friend Martinez in Guillaumin's Studio, 1878*

35½ x 29½ in.

AUGUSTE RENOIR (1841–1919)
98 · *Portrait of Claude Monet, 1872*
24¼ x 19¾ in.

AUGUSTE RENOIR

99 · *Madame Monet and Her Son in Their Garden at Argenteuil, 1874*

19¾ x 26¾ in.

AUGUSTE RENOIR
100 · *Head of a Dog, c.1870*
7⅞ x 8⅝ in.

AUGUSTE RENOIR
101 · *Regatta at Argenteuil, c.1874*
12¾ x 17⅞ in.

AUGUSTE RENOIR

102 · *Picking Flowers, c.1875*

21½ x 25¾ in.

AUGUSTE RENOIR

103 · *Portrait of the Artist's Friend, Georges Rivière, 1877*

14⅝ x 11⅝ in.

AUGUSTE RENOIR
104 · *The Young Soldier, c.1880*
21⅝ x 13 in.

AUGUSTE RENOIR
105 · *Young Woman Braiding Her Hair, 1876*
21 x 17½ in.

AUGUSTE RENOIR
106 · *The Artist's Son Jean Drawing, 1901*
17¾ x 21½ in.

AUGUSTE RENOIR

107 · *Child with Toys—Gabrielle and the Artist's Son Jean, c.1894*

21 ¼ x 24 ¾ in.

AUGUSTE RENOIR
108 · *Young Spanish Woman with a Guitar, 1898*
22 x 25 ½ in.

AUGUSTE RENOIR
109 · *The Fancy Hat, 1882-83*
21¾ x 18 in.

FREDERIC BAZILLE (1841–70)
110 · *The Artist's Studio, rue Visconti, Paris, 1867*
25½ x 19 in.

FRÉDÉRIC BAZILLE

III · *Portrait of Edmond Maître, 1869*

32½ x 25 in.

FRÉDÉRIC BAZILLE

112 · *The Ramparts at Aigues-Mortes, 1867*

23½ x 39½ in.

FRÉDÉRIC BAZILLE

113 · *Negro Girl with Peonies, 1870*

23¾ x 29¾ in.

HENRI ROUSSEAU (LE DOUANIER) (1844–1910)

114 · *View of the Ile Saint-Louis, Paris, in the Evening, c.1888*

18 x 21⅝ in.

DOUANIER ROUSSEAU

115 · *Banana Harvest, 1907–10*

14½ x 17¾ in.

DOUANIER ROUSSEAU
116 · *Still Life with Tropical Fruit, 1908*
25 ½ x 31 ¾ in.

DOUANIER ROUSSEAU

117 · *Tropical Landscape—An American Indian Struggling with an Ape, 1910*
44¾ x 64 in.

MARY CASSATT (1845–1926)
118 · *Child in a Straw Hat, c.1886*
25½ x 19¼ in.

MARY CASSATT
119 · *The Black Hat, pastel, c.1890*
24 x 18 in.

MARY CASSATT

120 · *Children Playing on the Beach, 1884*

38½ x 29¼ in.

MARY CASSATT

121 · *Little Girl in a Blue Armchair, 1878*

35 x 51 in.

PAUL GAUGUIN (1848–1903)

122 · *Still Life with Oysters, 1876*

21 x 36¾ in.

PAUL GAUGUIN

123 · *Still Life with Peonies, 1884*

23½ x 28¾ in.

PAUL GAUGUIN

124 · *Breton Girls Dancing, Pont-Aven, 1888*

28½ x 36¼ in.

PAUL GAUGUIN

125 · *Landscape at Le Pouldu, Brittany, 1890*

28⅞ x 36⅜ in.

PAUL GAUGUIN
126 · *Self-Portrait Dedicated to Carrière, c.1890–91*
16 x 12¾ in.

PAUL GAUGUIN

127 · Te Pape Nave Nave—*Delectable Waters, Tahiti, 1898*
29¼ x 37⅝ in.

JEAN-LOUIS FORAIN (1852–1931)
128 · *The Artist's Wife Fishing, c.1879*
37½ x 39½ in.

VINCENT VAN GOGH (1853–90)

129 · *Flower Beds in Holland, c.1883*

19⅛ x 26 in.

VINCENT VAN GOGH

130 · *The Bathing Float, Paris, c.1887*

7½ x 10⅝ in.

VINCENT VAN GOGH

131 · *Farmhouse in Provence, Arles, 1888*
18⅛ x 24 in.

VINCENT VAN GOGH

132 · *Daisies, Arles, 1888*

13⅛ x 16½ in.

VINCENT VAN GOGH

133 · *The Tree, Arles, September 1888*

$35\frac{3}{4}$ x 28 in.

VINCENT VAN GOGH

134 · *Still Life of Oranges and Lemons with Blue Gloves, Arles, January 1889*
18¾ x 24½ in.

VINCENT VAN GOGH

135 · *Green Wheat Fields, Auvers, July 1890*
28½ x 36 in.

GEORGES SEURAT (1859–91)
136 · *Peasant with a Hoe*, c.1882
5¾ x 9½ in.

GEORGES SEURAT
137 · *The Stone Breaker, c.1882*
5¾ x 9½ in.

GEORGES SEURAT
138 · *The Roadmenders, c.1882*
6⅛ x 9¾ in.

GEORGES SEURAT
139 · *Landscape with Houses, c.1882*
10⅞ x 18¼ in.

GEORGES SEURAT
140 · *Figures in a Landscape, c.1883*
6 x 9¾ in.

GEORGES SEURAT
141 · *The Watering Can—The Garden at Le Raincy, c.1883*
9¾ x 6 in.

GEORGES SEURAT

142 · *A Summer Landscape, 1883*

6¼ x 9⅞ in.

GEORGES SEURAT

143 · *The Lighthouse at Honfleur, 1886*

$26\frac{1}{4}$ x $32\frac{3}{8}$ in.

GEORGES SEURAT

144 · *The Seine, with Clothing on the Bank—Study for "Une Baignade,"* *1883–84*

6¾ x 10⅜ in.

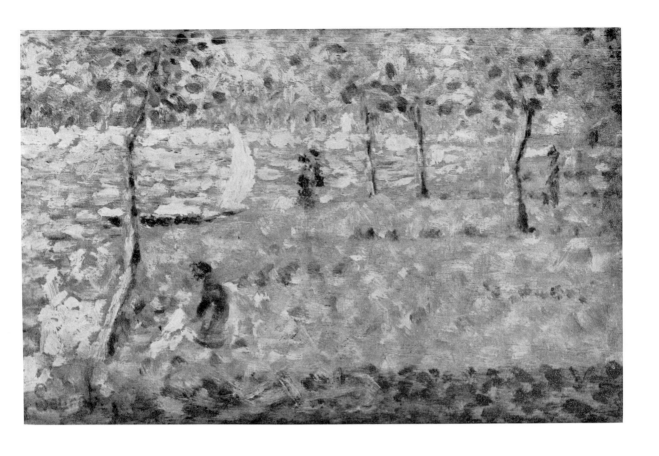

GEORGES SEURAT

145 · *The Bank of the Seine with Sailing Boat and Figures—*
Study for "La Grande Jatte," 1884–85
6½ x 9¾ in.

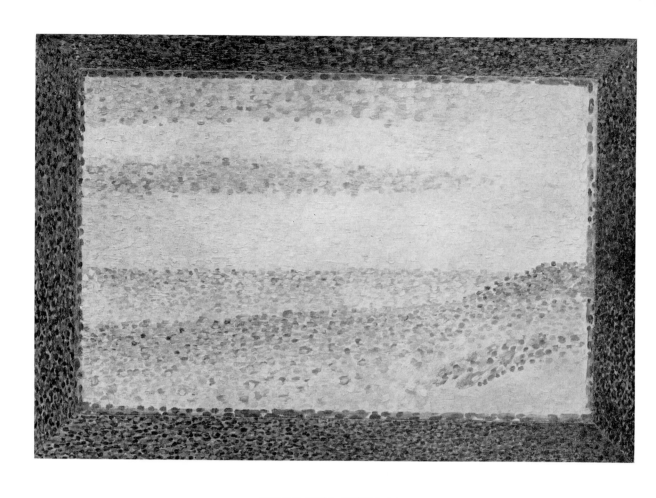

GEORGES SEURAT
146 · *Seascape (Gravelines), 1890*
8½ x 12 in.

HENRI DE TOULOUSE-LAUTREC (1864–1901)

147 · *The Artist's Dog, Flèche, Nice, 1881*

9¼ x 5½ in.

HENRI DE TOULOUSE-LAUTREC
148 · *Carmen (Carmen Gaudin)*, *c.1885*
9⅜ x 5⅞ in.

HENRI DE TOULOUSE-LAUTREC

149 · *The Bar, 1887*

21¾ x 16½ in.

HENRI DE TOULOUSE-LAUTREC

150 · *À la Bastille (Nini Peau de Chien)—The Absinthe Drinker (Jeanne Wenz), 1888*
$28\frac{1}{2}$ x $19\frac{1}{2}$ in.

HENRI DE TOULOUSE-LAUTREC

151 · *Red-Headed Woman in the Garden of Monsieur Forest, Montmartre, 1889*

28 x 23 in.

HENRI DE TOULOUSE-LAUTREC

152 · *At "Les Ambassadeurs" (Gens Chics), 1893*

31½ x 24½ in.

PIERRE BONNARD (1867-1947)
153 · *Paris, Rue de Parme on Bastille Day, 1890*
31¼ x 15¾ in.

PIERRE BONNARD
154 · *Two Dogs—Street in Eragny (Oise), c.1894*
13⅞ x 10⅝ in.

PIERRE BONNARD

155 · *The Cab Horse, Boulevard des Batignolles, Paris, c.1895*

11¾ x 15¾ in.

PIERRE BONNARD
156 · *Children Leaving School, c.1895*
11⅜ x 17½ in.

PIERRE BONNARD

157 · *The Artist's Sister, Madame Claude Terrasse, and Her Children, 1898*

12½ x 10½ in.

PIERRE BONNARD

158 · *Study for a Portrait of Vuillard, c.1910*

18 x 14¾ in.

PIERRE BONNARD

159 · *The Artist's Studio, Paris, 1900*

24¼ x 30 in.

PIERRE BONNARD
160 · *The Pont de Grenelle and the Eiffel Tower, c.1912*
21 ¼ x 27 in.

PIERRE BONNARD
161 · *Vase with Flowers, 1920*
17 x 15 in.

PIERRE BONNARD

162 · *Bouquet of Flowers, c.1926*

27½ x 18 in.

PIERRE BONNARD

163 · *The Barge "St. Tropez" in the Harbor of Cannes, 1926*
23½ x 25¼ in.

PIERRE BONNARD

164 · *The Open Window, c.1935*

15 x 18⅛ in.

PIERRE BONNARD

165 · *The Dining Room, c. 1930*

33 x 39½ in.

PIERRE BONNARD
166 · *The White Tablecloth, 1938-40*
32¼ x 30½ in.

PIERRE BONNARD

167 · *Nude in an Interior, c.1935*

52¾ x 27½ in.

PIERRE BONNARD

168 · *Stairs in the Artist's Garden, Le Cannet, 1942–44*

24⅞ x 28¾ in.

ÉDOUARD VUILLARD (1868–1940)
169 · *Self-Portrait, c.1891*
11 x 8½ in.

ÉDOUARD VUILLARD
170 · *Still Life, Bread and Jam, c.1888*
6 x 10 in.

ÉDOUARD VUILLARD
171 · *Child with Man Wearing a Red Scarf, c.1891*
11 7/8 x 7 1/4 in.

ÉDOUARD VUILLARD

172 · *Woman in Black Dress Standing Near a Table, c.1891*
10½ x 8⅝ in.

ÉDOUARD VUILLARD

173 · *Woman at Her Toilette, c.1891*

9¼ x 8⅝ in.

ÉDOUARD VUILLARD
174 · *The Conversation, 1891*
9⅜ x 13 in.

ÉDOUARD VUILLARD

175 · *The Yellow Curtain, c.1893*

13¾ x 15⅜ in.

ÉDOUARD VUILLARD

176 · *Still Life with the Artist's Paint Box and Moss Roses, 1898*

$14\frac{1}{4}$ x $16\frac{1}{2}$ in.

ÉDOUARD VUILLARD

177 · *Landscape of the Île-de-France, c.1894*

7⅜ x 10 in.

ÉDOUARD VUILLARD

178 · *Breakfast, 1894*

11 x 9⅜ in.

ÉDOUARD VUILLARD

179 · *Woman Sitting by the Fireside, c.1894*

8½ x 10¼ in.

ÉDOUARD VUILLARD

180 · *Two Women Drinking Coffee, c.1893*

$8\frac{1}{2}$ x $11\frac{1}{4}$ in.

ÉDOUARD VUILLARD
181 · *The Tuileries Gardens, Paris, 1897–1900*
15¼ x 13 in.

ÉDOUARD VUILLARD

182 · *Young Woman Trying on a Hat, c.1900*

16 x 12 in.

ÉDOUARD VUILLARD

183 · *Portrait of Madame Bonnard, 1895–1900*

16⅜ x 12½ in.

ÉDOUARD VUILLARD

184 · *The Bed, c. 1900*

16⅜ x 10⅝ in.

ÉDOUARD VUILLARD
185 · *The Artist's Mother Pouring Water into a Carafe, 1900-04*
17⅜ x 16⅛ in.

ÉDOUARD VUILLARD

186 · *Vase of Flowers on a Mantlepiece, c.1900*

14½ x 11¼ in.

ÉDOUARD VUILLARD

187 · *The Artist's Niece, Annette, in an Interior, c.1903*

24 x 26¼ in.

ÉDOUARD VUILLARD

188 · *Interior with a Man Reading, c. 1898,* gouache

$14\frac{1}{2}$ x $22\frac{7}{8}$ in.

ÉDOUARD VUILLARD
189 · *The Golden Chair, 1906*
26¾ x 26¼ in.

ÉDOUARD VUILLARD

190 · *Women Sewing, c.1912,* gouache

70¾ x 37¾ in.

ÉDOUARD VUILLARD

191 · *The Artist's Mother in Her Apartment, rue de Calais, Paris—Morning, c.1922*
17⅛ x 11¾ in.

HENRI MATISSE (1869–1954)

192 · *Still Life, c.1905*

7⅛ x 10⅛ in.

PABLO PICASSO (Born 1881)

193 · *Beach Scene, 1901*

11⅛ x 14 in.

PABLO PICASSO

194 · *The Death of Harlequin, gouache, 1905*

26 x 36½ in.

PABLO PICASSO

195 · *Harlequin on Horseback, 1904*

39⅜ x 27¼ in.

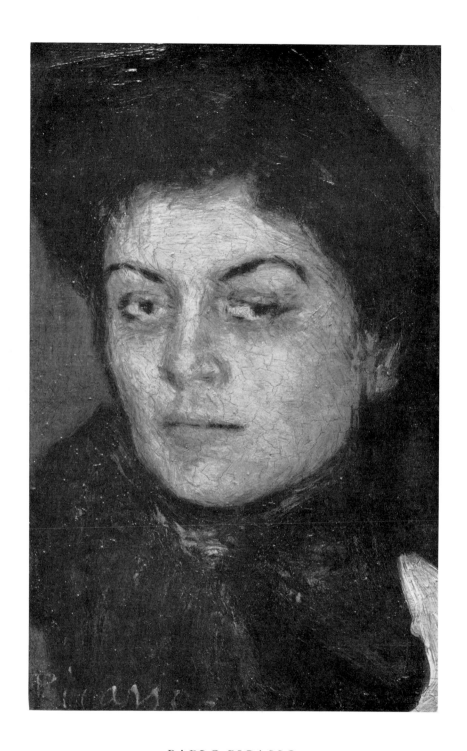

PABLO PICASSO
196 · *Portrait of the Artist's Sister, 1901*
13 7/8 x 8 3/4 in.

MAURICE UTRILLO (1883–1955)

197 · *The Pont Saint-Michel, Paris, c.1905*

18 x 21 in.

MAURICE UTRILLO

198 · *Row of Houses at Pierrefitte, c.1905*

10 x 13¼ in.

MAURICE UTRILLO
199 · *Landscape, Pierrefitte, c.1907*
10¼ x 13½ in.

MAURICE UTRILLO

200 · *Rue Cortot, Montmartre, 1909*
18⅛ x 13⅛ in.

MAURICE UTRILLO

201 · *The Church of St. Nicolas du Chardonnet, Paris, c.1911*

28¾ x 21¼ in.

MAURICE UTRILLO

202 · *Street in Sannois, c.1911*

21½ x 29¼ in.

WATERCOLORS
and
DRAWINGS

203 · CONSTANTIN GUYS (1802–92). The Duchess of Kent's State Carriage, c.1864(?). *Watercolor, 9½ x 15⅜ in.*

204 · CONSTANTIN GUYS. London Street Scene, c.1864(?). *Watercolor, 6⅞ x 10¾ in.*

205 · CONSTANTIN GUYS. The Lovers, c.1865. *Watercolor, 9⅜ x 6¼ in.*

206 · EUGÈNE BOUDIN. Four Ladies in Crinolines Walking, Trouville, 1865. *Watercolor,* 4½ x 9 in.

207 · EUGÈNE BOUDIN. On the Beach, 1865. *Watercolor,* 5⅜ x 8⅜ in.

208 · EUGÈNE BOUDIN. Crinolines on the Beach, 1865. *Watercolor,*
5¾ x 9¼ in.

209 · EUGÈNE BOUDIN. Conversation on the Beach, 1865. *Watercolor,*
4¼ x 5¾ in.

210 · EUGÈNE BOUDIN. Beach Tent with Flags, Trouville, c.1865. *Watercolor,* 7 x 12½ in.

211 · EUGÈNE BOUDIN. Conversation on the Beach with Six Figures, 1866. *Watercolor,* 6¾ x 10½ in.

212 · EUGÈNE BOUDIN. Afternoon on the Beach, 1865–66. *Watercolor,* 4¾ x 8½ in.

213 · EUGÈNE BOUDIN. Noon at Deauville, 1865–66. *Watercolor,* 5⅜ x 9⅛ in.

214 · EUGÈNE BOUDIN. Four Seated Ladies in Crinolines, Trouville, 1866. *Watercolor,* 4½ x 9 in.

215 · EUGÈNE BOUDIN. Beach Scene with Figures, 1865–66. *Watercolor,* 5¼ x 9 in.

216 · EUGÈNE BOUDIN. On the Beach, c.1866. *Watercolor,* 4⅛ x 6 in.

217 · EUGÈNE BOUDIN. Races at Deauville, 1866. *Watercolor,* 8 x 12¼ in.

218 · CAMILLE PISSARRO. Group of Trees, c.1865. *Charcoal,* 16⅜ x 23½ in.

219 · CAMILLE PISSARRO. The Road from Versailles to Louveciennes, c.1872. *Watercolor,* 7½ x 9⅞ in.

220 · ÉDOUARD MANET. The Railway Restaurant, c.1879(?). *Pen and ink, 7¾ x 11 in.*

221 · EDGAR DEGAS. The Artist's Brother, René, 1855.
Pencil, 12 x 9¼ in.

222 · EDGAR DEGAS. The Artist's Brother, René (Study for the Painting in the Smith College Museum of Art), 1855. *Pencil,* 11½ x 9 in.

223 · EDGAR DEGAS. Young Woman Embroidering (possibly the Artist's Sister, Marguerite), 1855–60. *Pencil,* 14 x 9¾ in.

224 · EDGAS DEGAS. Young Woman,
1861–65. *Oil on paper*, 6 x 5 in.

225 · EDGAR DEGAS. Race Horses—Study for "The Fallen Jockey," c.1865 (possibly
reworked later). *Charcoal*, 10⅞ x 17 in.

226 · EDGAR DEGAS. Studies of Horses, 1866–72(?). *Pencil,* 12¼ x 7½ in.

227 · EDGAR DEGAS. Huntsman Blowing His Horn, c.1872(?). *Pencil,* 7⅜ x 10¾ in.

228 · EDGAR DEGAS. Racehorses, 1875–77. *Pen and ink,* 4¼ x 6¾ in.

229 · EDGAR DEGAS. The Curtain, c.1881. *Pastel over Monotype*, 10¾ x 12¾ in.

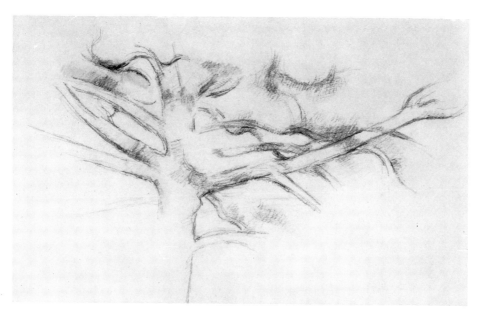

230 · PAUL CÉZANNE. Study of a Tree, 1885-90. *Pencil*, 9¾ x 16 in.

231 · PAUL CÉZANNE. Mont Sainte-Victoire Seen Beyond the Wall of the Jas de Bouffan, 1885–88. *Watercolor*, 18½ x 11¾ in.

232 · ALFRED SISLEY. The Seine at Auteuil, 1876–77. *Pen and ink,*
6 x 8 in.

233 · ODILON REDON. Butterflies, c.1912. *Watercolor,*
10½ x 8 in.

234 · BERTHE MORISOT. At the Edge of the Forest, c.1874.
Watercolor, 7½ x 8⅝ in.

235 · BERTHE MORISOT. The Artist's Sister,
Edma, 1864. *Watercolor,* 10½ x 6½ in.

236 · BERTHE MORISOT. The Artist's Sister, Edma, with Her Daughter, Jeanne, 1872. *Watercolor,* 9 x 8¼ in.

237 · AUGUSTE RENOIR. The Milliner, c.1879. *Pencil*, 16½ x 10¾ in.

238 · AUGUSTE RENOIR. Young Woman Standing, c.1880. *Crayon*,
17¼ x 9¾ in.

239 · VINCENT van GOGH. Harvest—The Plain of La Crau, Arles, June 1888. *Reed pen and ink, 9½ x 12¾ in.*

240 · VINCENT van GOGH. Ploughman in the Fields near Arles, 1888–89. *Reed pen and ink, 10 x 13½ in.*

241 · GEORGES SEURAT. Woman with a Bouquet, c.1882. *Conté crayon*, 12 x 9¼ in.

242 · GEORGES SEURAT. Peasant Woman Bending, c.1882. *Conté crayon,* 9⅜ x 6½ in.

243 · GEORGES SEURAT. Street Cleaner with Hose, c.1883. *Conté crayon,* 12⅛ x 9⅜ in.

244 · HENRI de TOULOUSE-LAUTREC. The Carriage, c.1880. *Sepia ink,*
12¼ x 17⅛ in.

245 · ÉDOUARD VUILLARD. Woman in Bed, c.1891. *Watercolor,* 6 x 8¾ in.

246 · PABLO PICASSO. Self-Portrait, c.1901. *Crayon and wash,* 12 x 9½ in.

Collection Mrs. Mellon Bruce:

Catalogue numbers 1, 16, 18, 27, 29, 33, 34, 37, 38, 45, 52, 53, 61, 66, 71, 72, 75, 80, 82, 84, 86, 92, 93, 95, 99, 100, 101, 102, 103, 105, 108, 120, 131, 145, 147, 148, 154, 155, 156, 157, 162, 168, 171, 172, 173, 174, 175, 176, 178, 179, 180, 186, 192, 198, 199, 200, 203, 235, 236, 238, 245, 246.

The remaining paintings and drawings are from the collection of Mr. and Mrs. Paul Mellon.

H. K. PRESS

WASHINGTON